Gangs and Violence

TOOKIE SPEAKS OUT AGAINST GANG VIOLENCE™

Stanley "Tookie" Williams
with Barbara Cottman Becnel

The Rosen Publishing Group's
PowerKids Press™
New York

Published in 1996 by The Rosen Publishing Group, Inc.
29 East 21st Street, New York, NY 10010

First Edition

Book design: Kim Sonsky

Photo credits: Front cover © Dusty Willison/International Stock; front cover inset, back cover and p. 4 © J. Patrick Forden; pp. 7, 12 by Kim Sonsky; pp. 8, 15 © Douglas Burrows/The Gamma Liaison Network; p. 11 © Dario Perla/International Stock; p. 16 © Ray Solowinski/International Stock; p. 19 by Michael Brandt; p. 20 © James Davis/International Stock.

Williams, Stanley.
    Gangs and violence / by Stanley "Tookie" Williams and Barbara Cottman Becnel.
        p.   cm. — (Tookie speaks out against gang violence)
    Includes index.
    Summary: A founder of the Crips in Los Angeles introduces kids to the dangers of belonging to a gang.
        ISBN 0-8239-2345-2
        1. Gangs—United States—Juvenile literature. 2. Violent crimes—United States—Juvenile literature. 3. Juvenile delinquency—United States—Juvenile literature. 4. Crips (Gang)—Juvenile literature. [1. Gangs. 2. Crips (Gang). 3. Juvenile delinquency.] I. Becnel, Barbara Cottman. II. Title. III. Series: Williams, Stanley. Tookie speaks out against gang violence.

HV6789.W5 1996
364.1'06'6—dc20

95-51329
CIP
AC

Manufactured in the United States of America

Contents

1 My First Fight   5

2 Little Bullies, Big Bullies   6

3 The Crips   9

4 Violence All Day   10

5 Gangbangers   13

6 Losing Buddha   14

7 Being a Gangbanger Is No Fun   17

8 An Important Lesson   18

9 Living By Good Rules   21

10 Don't Be a Follower   22

   Glossary   23

   Index   24

My First Fight

I was named after my father, Stanley Williams. His parents nicknamed him "Tookie." By the time I was a teenager, most people called me Tookie too.

I was born in Shreveport, Louisiana, but was brought up in South Central Los Angeles. My mother and I took a bus from Shreveport to Los Angeles when I was about seven. My parents were divorced.

The first time I explored my new neighborhood, I ran into a **bully** (BUL-lee), Monroe. He punched me real hard. We got into a fight.

Tookie learned violence from the gang members in his neighborhood.

Little Bullies, Big Bullies

Monroe wanted me to be afraid of him. That's why he hit me. Bullies use **violence** (VY-o-lents) to scare other kids into doing what they want them to do. I won the fight with Monroe that day. But I really lost, because after the fight I decided that pushing other kids around was the best way to feel good about myself. I became a bully, just like Monroe.

Soon I found out there were many young bullies in my neighborhood. They grew up to be big bullies and gang members. So did I.

Bullies use violence to try to ▶ feel good about themselves.

The Crips

I saw a lot of violence when I was a kid. Gang members always started fights while hanging around my school and neighborhood.

At first, I didn't belong to a gang, so I had no one to protect me. I fought the gangs alone. Then, when I was 17, I met Raymond Washington. We created a gang called the Crips. We started the Crips to protect ourselves and our families from other gangs. We used violence against their violence. But starting the Crips only made things worse.

◀ *Gang members often make up hand signals to tell other people who they are or what gang they belong to.*

Violence All Day

Most Crips became **weightlifters** (WAYT-lif-ters) as soon as they joined our gang. We lifted weights to make our muscles big for when we had to fight others. Back then, Crips didn't use guns. We fought only with our fists.

Crips were good fighters. We were very strong because of our weightlifting. Few people could beat us. So other gangs began using guns to protect themselves from us. Now our lives were full of violence from morning to night. Starting the Crips had caused more violence, not less.

In the past, it was important for gang members to be strong enough to fight with their fists. Now they use guns. ▶

Gangbangers

Our violence earned us a nickname. We were called **gangbangers** (GANG-bang-erz). A gangbanger is a gang member who "bangs"—or hits—people. He uses his fists, or a gun, or a knife, to make other people do what he wants. Gangbangers also use violence when they do bad things like sell drugs or steal cars or take money that doesn't belong to them.

Gangbangers are always trying to prove that they're **down** (DOWN), really tough guys.

◄ *Gangbangers hurt other people to get what they want.*

Losing Buddha

Gangbangers hurt others. But they also get hurt. That's true because violence attracts more violence. The saddest day of my life was when Buddha, my best **homeboy** (HOME-boi)—or friend—was killed by gun-shots. A kid who was scared of Buddha shot him dead. Buddha was a gangbanger just like me.

Years later, I got shot too. My leg bones were shattered by the bullets. Doctors said I would never walk again. It took a long time to recover, but now I can walk again.

Gang violence hurts many people, both gang members and others. ▶

Being a Gangbanger Is No Fun

It's no fun being a gangbanger. Gang-bangers are always looking over their shoulders because they're afraid someone may hurt them. Gangbangers also worry about getting caught by the police for doing bad things like stealing.

Many gangbangers are scared all the time. But they won't tell anyone because they want their homeboys to think they're down. It's truly no fun being a gangbanger.

Gangbangers scare everyone in their neighborhood.

17

An Important Lesson

Many of my homeboys have been killed. It feels terrible. But I have learned something important. When you use violence to boss other kids around, or to take what doesn't belong to you, you're not really proving that you're strong or tough.

If you were tough and strong, you could tell your homeboys the truth about how you feel. You could admit when you're scared. You could say no to violence. And you would not let another homeboy push you into doing something you know is wrong.

Kids who are truly tough and strong don't need violence to prove it. ▶

Living By Good Rules

Gangbangers live by bad rules. Their rules make it okay to be dishonest. That's why gangbangers act like they're tough when they're really afraid. Their rules make it okay to use violence against others. And their rules also make it okay for gang-bangers to put their own lives in danger.

You don't have to live by those rules. You can choose to live by new rules, good rules that don't hurt you or other kids.

◀ *Choosing to live by good rules, such as staying in school, will help keep you safe from danger.*

Don't Be a Follower

When you get into trouble by doing the bad things you see your homeboys do, you're being a **follower** (FOL-low-er). A follower does what his homeboys tell him to do. A follower lives by rules that he doesn't make.

Don't be a follower. Start telling yourself that you will never be a gangbanger. If you are already a gangbanger, start looking for a new group of friends that won't push you to be violent. When you're a **leader** (LEE-der)—not a follower—you make the rules that *you* live by.

Glossary

bully (BUL-lee) Person who uses violence to scare other people.

to be **down** (DOWN) To be ready to do anything, no matter how dangerous or how bad.

follower (FOL-low-er) Person who does what other people tell him to do.

gangbanger (GANG-bang-er) Gang member who uses violence to make other people do what he wants.

homeboy (HOME-boi) Friend or partner.

leader (LEE-der) Person who lives by his own rules and sets an example for others.

violence (VY-o-lents) Hurting yourself or others.

weightlifter (WAYT-lif-ter) Someone who lifts weights to increase his strength and muscles.

Index

B
bully, 5,6

C
Crips, 9, 10

D
death, 14, 18
down, to be, 13, 17

F
fear, 6, 17, 18, 21
follower, 22

G
gang, 6, 9,10
gangbangers, 13, 14, 17, 21, 22
guns, 10, 13, 14

H
homeboy, 14, 17, 18, 22

L
leader, 22

R
rules, bad, 21, 22

S
stealing, 13, 17

V
violence, 6, 9, 10, 13, 14, 18, 21, 22

W
weightlifters, 10